CLICKETY CLACK, CLICKETY CLACK

MB MACAW BOOKS

© Macaw Books

www.macawbooks.com

Printed in India

Every morning, the train pulled out of the station. 'Clickety clack, clickety clack!' sang its wheels on the railway track.

It was orange and green in colour, with an orange and blue engine. How cheerful it looked, as it drove through the city buildings!

The train was travelling to the mountains. It was taking its passengers from the hot city to the cool mountains.

Among the passengers, was one very excited little girl named Cady.
She had never been on a train before.

Cady was travelling with her Mummy, Daddy and pet cat named Grace. Cady and Grace could not stop staring out of the window.

'There is so much to see!' said Cady. She loved to watch the cities and towns as the train passed through them.

There were sandwiches, cakes and bread sticks on the train.

There was Cady's favourite sweet corn soup too.

'Yumm!' said Cady, happily. It was wonderful to eat delicious food while watching the view from the train!

The train sped through green valleys and farmlands. 'Hello!' Cady cried to the roosters in the farm.

'Hello!' she cried to the little farm boy. He smiled and waved back at her.

The train had twenty coaches. 'Clickety clack, clickety clack!' came the sound as the train drove over hills, and crossed a waterfall. How beautiful it was!

There was a tiny house below waterfall too. Smoke was coming out of its chimney. 'How nice to live by a waterfall!' said Cady.

The train whistled through tea gardens. The workers in the gardens smiled at the passengers on the train.

'I see a windmill!' said Cady, 'And some sheep and goats!' She enjoyed spotting different animals and plants from the train.

The train reached its destination after a few hours, and Cady loved every minute of her journey. She could not wait for the train journey back!

ACROSS RIVERS
AND SEAS

Joe was taking a boat ride across the river. 'I have never taken a boat ride before!' said Joe to the boatman. He was so excited!

'Well then,' replied the boatman, 'I am sure you will love the water. Let us row!' And so, the boatman began to row while Joe admired the world around him.

The boat was small. It could hold only two people, but it easily carried the weight of its passengers. Joe loved how the little boat rocked gently in the river.

At first the boat set out slowly through the water. It moved steadily away from land and soon the boat was surrounded by water on all sides.

After some time, the boatman stopped rowing and said, 'What a great spot to catch some fish!' He took out a fishing rod with the bait and gave it to Joe.

How excited Joe was! He whipped the fishing line into the water and waited excitedly. Soon, Joe felt a tug on his fishing line. He pulled up the line and he had caught a fish!

They rowed to the point where the river flows into the sea. 'Look!' cried Joe, 'We are rowing into the sea!'

And so they rowed from the
river into the sea. Joe kept an
eye out for sharks and dolphins.

After a while, Joe noticed a little creature in the water. It was swimming on its back. 'What is that?' Joe pointed. 'Let us find out,' replied the boatman.

And it was a little otter! It looked up at them queerly and then dived back into the water. 'Goodbye, dear otter!' called Joe, and on they rowed.

They rowed until they reached a spot where there was lots of colourful seaweed under the water.

'Look!' cried Joe, 'There are small colourful fishes among it too!'
They rowed happily through the beautiful seaweed patches.

The sea water pushed and pulled the boat. And there were large waves running through the water. The boat moved bumpily, and Joe clapped with every lurch.

And now it was time to row back home. What a great day they had on the water! 'I love the river so much!' said Joe, 'Let us return soon again!'

www.ingramcontent.com/pod-product-compliance
Lightning Source LLC
LaVergne TN
LVHW082324080426

835508LV00042B/1535